W9-BGN-442

Learn'Em Good
-Social Skills-

Simple and Effective Ways to Improve Your Child's Social Skills in School and at Home

Stuart Ackerman MSc.Ed, B.A.
Learn'Em Good Publishing

Improve Your Child's Social Skills

Improve Your Child's Social Skills

Watch for the following Learn'Em Good books:

Learn'Em Good Writing
Learn'Em Good Math
Learn'Em Good Reading
Learn'Em Good Grammar
Learn'Em Good Homeschooling
Learn'Em Good Learning Disabilities
Learn'Em Good ADD/ADHD
Learn'Em Good Study Skills
Learn'Em Good Geometry
Learn'Em Good Fractions
Learn'Em Good Math - Number Sense

Introduction............11
Part 1 – Social Skills at School

Continued...

Part 2 – Social Skills at Home

Continued...

Continued...

Part 3- Charts and Check-lists

Improve Your Child's Social Skills

Introduction
All about Social Skills

What is the issue?

Social skills are those communication and friendship-keeping abilities that allow children to maintain and grow healthy relationships with their peers.

Children's friendships are often in limbo. Some kids consistently have good friends while some kids drop old ones for new ones. Unfortunately, some children don't seem to have the ability to cultivate friends at all.

As parents and teachers, it is important for us to help these children who don't seem to have the ability to develop meaningful friendships. Reason being, these children miss out on opportunities to learn social skills that will be important throughout their lives. More and more, the field of Emotional Intelligence (EQ), which consists of social skills, is revealing the importance of social skills as indicators of future success (sometimes more so than IQ). These skills involve effective communication, conflict resolution skills, and healthy social relationships. Not only do these kids miss out on social development, but they also seem to have underdeveloped self confidence and self esteem.

These children, without proper social connections, may feel a lack of connection with others. They might begin to resent the education system which may result in dropping out, lack of effort, poor grades, mental health issues, and delinquent behaviour.

Today's schools are focusing more and more on 'team activities' and 'group learning'. Even children in the primary grades are often placed in group situations whereby they must learn to work with others towards a common learning goal. This poses a great problem for children who have not yet developed their social skills.

Why are there problems?

According to the Eric Digest, some children behave in an aggressive or disruptive manner and, hence, are rejected by peers. Other children withdraw from peer interactions and, in this way, limit their ability to gain acceptance and friendship (Coie and Kupersmidt 1983; Dodge 1983). Each type of ineffective social behavioral pattern can stem from different root causes. One possible cause is a lack of knowledge about effective interaction strategies. Another potential cause relates to the children's emotional states. Academic problems also can contribute to ineffective social behavior. Children who cannot engage themselves with classroom work assignments often disrupt and irritate their peers. Similarity fosters social acceptance. Conversely, children tend to encounter social rejection when they are perceived to be dissimilar from their peers. This may occur when children are of a different ethnic group or sex, are physically unattractive or physically or mentally challenged, or are newcomers to their classrooms (Asher and others 1982). Family problems can have damaging effects on children's peer relations. For example, children of divorcing parents may act out feelings of anger at school, eliciting rejection from peers in the process.

Regardless of the reasons, your will be able to help your child improve his or her communication, problem-solving, and friendship-maintaining skills by following the strategies in this book.

The first section of this book presents social difficulties your child may have at school and strategies you can use to help your child. The second section contains possible social difficulties your child may be having at home, and again, effective strategies you can use at home to help your child. The last section in this book contains useful resources such as charts and tracking sheets you can use in order to motivate and reinforce your child to improve his or her social skills.

Good luck, and Learn'Em Good!

Part 1-

Social Skills at School

Bothers Others in Class

Let's face it, who wants to admit that their own child bothers others? We, as parents, don't want to 'see' that our own child might be the problem. Unfortunately, denying that our own child is a problem won't help him.

It is difficult for us to help our child change his/her behavior especially if we are not physically there in the classroom. There are ways, though, that you can help your child interact appropriately in the classroom without being there.

- Write a contract with your child incorporating behavioral expectations, rewards, and punishments. Have your child play an active part in designing the contract.

- Have your child be a partner in the process. Your child should take responsibility for his own actions. How else is he going to become responsible to improve his behaviour if he doesn't fess up to his problem areas?

- Teach your child to monitor his own behaviour. Ask him exactly what happened in class and discuss with him what was wrong with his behaviour and how he 'should' have acted.

- Try to 'catch' your child acting inappropriately when you and your child are with family and friends with children. If you can catch him interacting inappropriately, stop him and discuss the situation. This will reinforce behaviors in the classroom.

- Enrol your child in an after school activity that promotes discipline such as martial arts, music, structured sports and so on.

- Communicate with your child's teacher. Have your child's teacher write a note to you about your child's good and 'not so good' social behaviour. Make sure that you praise and/or reward your child for proper socialization and deliver consequences (that you drafted in your contract with your child) if he bothers others.

- Try to purchase books that illustrate how inappropriate social behaviours can be corrected. For younger students, I prefer Franklin and Berenstain Bears books.

- If you really want to make a serious effort, do some role playing scenarios with your child. Involve other kids and family members.

- Be a good role model. When you are with your child and other adults, point out to your child how you interact with your friends.

It is understandable that it's hard to admit that our own child is the problem. It's more important though, to accept it and correct it.

Choosing the Right Friends at School

Having social skills difficulties usually involves difficulties interpreting social cues.

Your child, although he or she genuinely wants to find compatible friends, may have a problem picking the right friends in school. Your child may need some guidance on how to choose an appropriate friend.

Sit down with your child and discuss what characteristics a good friend should have (you can use the chart in the resource section in this book). Try to get your child to say (and write down if you prefer) such qualities as honesty, compassion, caring, includes others, etc. Conversely, have your child do the same for a person who would not be a good friend (e.g. a liar, excludes others, calls names, etc.). Tell your child that next time, at school, he or she should think about these qualities when making a new friend or deciding to keep or get rid of another.

Lastly, have your child invite friends over for play dates. You can observe your child's interaction with the friend. Try to determine the positive and/or negative qualities your child's friend has. Then, point those qualities out to your child. Unfortunately, your child may not be able to see the friend's positive and/or negative qualities on his or her own.

By teaching your child about the various personality traits and how to find them, you will help your child choose the right friends at school.

Class and Recess Leader

Your child may find him or herself as a leader for a group project in the class or as the leader for a game of soccer at recess time. Regardless of the situation, your child will need the appropriate leadership skills in order to effectively socialize with peers. If your child has a history of not being a good leader (e.g. bossy and mean) you may want to consider having a discussion at home.

If your child is leading a group project in class it would be a good idea to go over the attributes of a good leader. Make it clear to your child that a good leader is fair and has to follow the rules. Quite often, teachers will give each student in a group a specific job. If that is the case, tell your child that he or she has to follow the teacher's guidelines. Your child's job, as leader, is to make sure that everyone else is doing his or her job. Make it very clear to your child that this does not mean that he or she should be bossy (you might want to model the difference between delegating a job as opposed to bossiness to your child). Your child should also be aware of the fact that if everyone in the group decides on their role, your child's job is to respect the other children by listening and being fair if possible (again, you may want to model this type of situation at home).

Your child may also find him or herself in charge of the soccer game at recess time. Try to reinforce similar 'leader' characteristics to your child. With this situation though, make it clear to your child that this situation will dictate future social interactions. That is, if your child is unfair (i.e. making teams or rules), other kids won't want to play with him in the future. Discuss with your child how to be fair if he or she is the leader of a game or activity. Ask your child how he or she would feel if someone else was the leader and made teams and rules that your child didn't like.

Improve Your Child's Social Skills

Finally, remember to let your child know that if he or she is a fair leader, the other kids won't mind if your child is the leader again sometime whereas if your child is an unfair leader, other kids will play with someone else in the future.

You may want to consider letting your child be the 'leader' for a specific family outing (e.g. dinner and a movie night). This will allow you to monitor your child's leadership skills (i.e. he may be bossy, she might not listen to suggestions) and correct them if need be.

Conflict – My Child is Often in Conflict

It is common for students who are often in conflict require some social interaction skills and perhaps some anger management techniques.

Every child has his or her own reasons for being in conflict. Sometimes it is due to academic frustration, issues at home, low self esteem issues, or simply a lack of understanding of social cues and interaction.

You can help your child resolve and avoid conflicts.

1. Evaluate your child's conflict resolution techniques. Find out if your child is misreading social cues or has difficulty managing his/her emotions.

2. Show your child how to solve conflicts. Do some role playing at home. Be a role model by pointing out your conflicts and how you solve them.

3. Make sure your child understands natural consequences from his/her actions (i.e. if he/she is in conflict, others won't want to play or interact with your child).

4. Teach your child how to stop, take a step back, and think about the situation before reacting. Often, students have difficulty with self-monitoring.

5. Write a contract with your child. You can both decide on rewards and consequences for appropriate and inappropriate conflict resolutions (see the sheet in the resource section in this book).

6. Teach your child how to resolve conflicts. Your child may not know how to properly solve different types of conflicts. Explain how different situations require different solutions. Be as specific as you can.

Quite often, we take for granted that our children know how to resolve conflicting issues just because we know how to do it ourselves. You have to show your child how to solve conflicts, reinforce wanted behaviours, and follow up with praise.

Conflict Resolution at School

At home, you can guide your child through conflict resolutions because you are there with your child. At school, it's a different story since you are not physically present.

You can use the following strategies to help your child solve conflicts at school. Have your child practice these strategies at home by doing some role play.

1. **Know the situation**. Your child must first understand the problem. He has to express his feelings and listen to the other person in order to fully comprehend the situation.
2. **Avoid more trouble**. Make sure your child doesn't add fuel to the fire. Your child should avoid name calling and physical confrontations. If need be, have your child not say a word for ten seconds while taking deep breaths to cool off.
3. **Use 'I' statements**. In order to keep the conflict civil and non-offensive, have your child refrain from saying, "You shouldn't have..." Instead, have your child say, "I feel..." This will eliminate the 'blame game' which often makes things worse.
4. **Find a solution**. Let your child know that both parties should agree on a solution that is fair to both.

Set up some possible scenarios at home that your child can practice with via role play. You can have your child practice conflict resolution skills with family members or friends when they come over.

Constantly Annoying Others

The main reason why children constantly annoy other kids is due to their desire for attention. Unfortunately, this attention is negative. I most children's eyes, if they can't get any positive attention, then negative attention is the next best thing. The best way to deal with your child's constant annoying behavior towards others is to teach your child how to seek positive attention.

The first step is to discuss with your child the difference between appropriate and inappropriate social behaviors. Once your child can verbalize that he or she knows the difference, you can begin to discuss the concept of attention. Tell your child that there is a difference between positive attention and negative attention. Let your child know that positive attention from positive actions (e.g. including others, speaking nicely, sharing, etc) results in other kids wanting to be friends and play with your child. Conversely, your child should be aware that negative attention from negative actions (e.g. name calling, exclusion, stealing, pestering, etc) results in other kids not wanting to be friends and not wanting to play with your child.

You can also show your child how others react to negative behaviors while watching television or reading a book. You can ask your child how he knows that a character is bothering another character. Then, have your child explain how the person or character being bothered feels about the one who is doing the bothering. You can also do some role play in your home in order to clearly show your child how to attain positive attention from peers.

Finally, make sure that family members give your child positive attention. It is best to eliminate all negative attention, that is, completely ignore inappropriate negative attention seeking behaviors. Over time, your child will learn that the only attention he or she gets is positive.

Cooperative Classroom Assignments

Cooperative group projects can create peer acceptance of children who are trying to improve their social situation, including children who are seen as different by their classmates. Under these conditions, teachers assign interesting tasks to small work groups. The group members must work cooperatively to achieve the tasks. In so doing, they must interact with peers they would typically avoid and discover new reasons for liking them.

In every classroom I have taught (and most teachers in the public system would agree), I have had as much if not more, students working in groups than individually. I've had students work on science projects, reading stories, answering questions, and completing math assignments in small groups. My proof that this was always a good teaching and learning strategy was due to the fact that there were often group interaction 'problems'. This is clear that students do in fact require social skills practice in small groups.

You can have some input with regards to your child being placed in cooperative classroom groups. That is, even though most teachers create the groups or let the kids choose, you can have a say. Kindly ask your child's teacher to place your child in heterogeneous groups when possible. This way, your child won't be working with the same kids all the time. You can also create a reward system with your child so that every time he or she works well with other kids in the class there's some incentive (see the charts in the resource section).

Dealing with Aggressive Kids

The first issue you should deal with when your child feels that another child is aggressive (i.e. a bully) is to make sure that your child understands that it is not your child's fault. Often, children internalize feelings of low self worth when they are picked on. Explain to your child that the aggressive child is behaving this way because he or she feels better about him or herself by picking on others, or that his or her upbringing wasn't very good, and so on.

Help your child develop problem solving techniques by thinking of ways to deal with the aggressive child. Try to get your child to tell you that the problem can be solved by telling a teacher, yourself, or even talking to the bully. If your child feels that telling on the aggressive child will only lead to more aggressive behavior (i.e. due to tattling), remind your child that the bullying won't stop unless an adult knows about it.

Quite often, as you probably already know, kids who bully are often those who have low self esteem. They target other kids who seem to have even lower self esteem because they are easy targets. If this is the case for your child, you might want to consider taking some steps to improve your child's self esteem. Personally, and professionally, I believe that nothing beats martial arts. The amount of confidence, self esteem, and feeling of self worth a child can attain from martial arts is unparalleled (not to mention the ability to defend oneself). If this is not your child's cup of tea, consider another activity that your child will enjoy and do well at, and at the same time, improve his or her self-esteem.

Deals with Winning and Accepts Losing

I've seen it in the classroom, in gym class, and in the school yard. Some kids are poor winners and sore losers. Unfortunately, they don't take other children's feelings into consideration after playing.

If you have seen your child win or lose in an inappropriate fashion, you should make your child aware of how others feel. The best way to do so is to catch your child in the act. That is, catch the moment your child loses or wins and determine if he or she is a poor winner or sore loser.

If you catch your child winning a game, and hopefully the other child being a poor loser, point out to your child how the other child is behaving. Have your child express to you that he doesn't want to be nor play with the other child because of the other child's attitude (i.e. being a sore loser). Let your child know that that's the way your child looks when he or she is a sore loser (i.e. no one wants to be around your child nor play with your child). Conversely, if your child loses a game and another child is a poor winner, ask your child the similar questions. Get your child to verbalize that the other child is making your child feel bad.

Let your child know that this is how she or he sometimes behaves. Have your child explain and show you how he or she will act in the future so that other kids would still want to play with and be with your child.

Difficulty Making Friends

As a parent, my heart goes out to other parents who come to the realization that their child doesn't have any friends at school.

As a teacher, I see this trend far too often. Many times, I have seen children standing near the school wall outside at recess time, playing by themselves. It is often the 'new' student who comes a new school, state, province, or even country, who has a difficult time adjusting

There are several factors that are responsible for this type of situation. Usually, this problem is just a matter of a child not using the appropriate social skills or a lack in self confidence.

If this is your situation, the first step to take is to talk to your child's teacher. It is important to find out if your child is attempting to socialize. Is your child trying to make friends or is he keeping to himself?

If your child is shy, or lacking in confidence, then perhaps you might consider the following:

1. Enroll your child in an extra-curricular program in the school. This will give your child a chance to socialize with his/her peers and classmates during a fun activity.

2. Enroll your child in an after school activity such as martial arts, swimming, or music. These activities are non-competitive. This will give your child the opportunity to measure himself against himself as opposed to measuring himself against others. This can be a real confidence booster for children who always compare themselves to other kids.

3. You can also take the initiative by getting the phone number of some children in your child's class and inviting

24

them over for a play day. This will help your child in several ways. First, it will model the behavior that you want your child to demonstrate. You will be showing your child that he or she has to take the initiative to get together with friends. Secondly, it will give other children the opportunity to see your child in a different atmosphere that will show a more positive side of your child's personality. Lastly, it will allow your child to interact with others in his own home. This will add an extra comfort level for your child thus giving him more confidence to interact socially.

Try these strategies and see which works best for your child. Remember, children don't have the socializing experiences that we do. We have to give them the opportunities to practice their social skills and guide them to interact appropriately with their peers.

Disruptive to Others in the Class

Quite often, children who don't have well developed social skills lack the ability to empathize. These kids aren't able to put themselves in other kids' shoes.

Your child may, in school, find himself in trouble by the teacher or, have another student angry at him for being disruptive. The first thing you must do is point out what your child is doing wrong (he may not be aware of what he is doing). Ask your child what would disturb him if he was trying to work in the classroom (look for answers such as: someone talking, making sounds, and shuffling papers). Have your child determine the disruptive behaviors that he does in class. Ask your child how he thinks other kids feel about it. Let your child know that other kids will be upset and/or angry with him and may not want to play with him.

Then, have your child think of ways to be less disruptive (e.g. don't talk to kids when they are working, whisper if he has to talk to someone else, don't shuffle papers during quiet work time, wait for a better time such as recess to socialize, sharpen a pencil before it is quiet work time).

You can ask your child's teacher to remind your child to not be disruptive when it is quiet working time. Your child's teacher can use a hand signal so that your child knows when he or she should be quiet. You can also write down (see the 'disturbing others' chart in the resource section) or print out a note that your child can keep at his or her desk reminding your child to respect others during independent work time.

Expressing Anger

Students who have anger management difficulties usually find themselves as outcasts in the classroom. Other students see 'angry' kids as 'walking time bombs' who should be avoided.

I have dealt with many students in the past who have had difficulty controlling their anger. On many occasions, I have spoken to the other students in the class to try to get them to include the 'angry' student. As expected, I always received the same answer. The other kids in the class said that they didn't want to work with the 'angry' student because these kids didn't want to get yelled at. They felt as if they were walking on eggshells because they always had to watch what they said and did. If your child has a severe anger management issue, you should probably seek professional help. If your child has mild difficulties with controlling his or her anger, you can use some strategies to help.

The first thing your child should do is understand why he or she is angry. At home, you can discuss possible situations at school that could cause your child to become angry. After your child becomes aware of the possible situations, make him or her aware of how other kids feel when they are yelled at or when they are the recipients of foul language from your child. Ask your child how he or she would feel in the same situation. Finally, help your child brainstorm alternative ways to respond to situations that would make your child angry. You may also want to set up a reward system at home (see the charts in the resource section of this book). First, have your child sit down with you to set up a reward system whereby every day your child appropriately expresses his or her anger. In the chart, he or she can receive a sticker (or check mark). With your child, decide upon a reasonable reward for a reasonable number of days of the proper expression of anger. You may also choose to remove stickers or check marks for days that your child inappropriately expresses his or her anger.

Extra-Curricular Activities

One of the most important ways you can improve your child's social life and skills is to have him or her participate in extra-curricular activities especially at school.

In the classroom, kids interact with each other in a different manner than during after school activities. When school ends, and it is fun time (not to say that the classroom isn't fun), children behave differently with one another. They are not confined to the rules and expectations of the classroom. Rather, they can let loose and have more fun. This would be an opportune time for your child to socialize and interact with peers and classmates.

After school, or extra-curricular activities, can involve a sport, group games, crafts, or play activities. During this time, your child will be interacting with other children who are generally interested in the same activities as your child. There will be a common interest that your child and other children can share, therefore there will be a reduction in competition.

You can encourage your child to initiate conversation with some of the other children during the extra-curricular activity. Make your child aware that he or she will have similar interests and common goals as the other kids in the program. This would be a good time to start to develop relationships with other kids in the school, and especially, other kids in the class.

Fulfilling a Role within the Group

As a teacher, I have witnessed many students neglect and/or ignore their role during group work. Not only does this behavior decrease the chances on your child receiving a good grade, but it also prevents your child from developing the appropriate 'group' skills he or she needs. Whether your child is given the role as leader, follower, scribe, or observer, he or she must adhere to the teacher's instructions and fulfill the appropriate role.

At home, you can explain to your child the dynamics and importance of group work. For example, explain to your child that everyone in the group has a role and in order to do the assignment and get a good grade, everyone must do their own job. Tell your child that he or she is given a job by the teacher and should follow the instructions, regardless if your child likes the role or not. *being responsible*

Draw some parallels for your child. Point out that everyone in the house has his and/or her role. Someone in the house cooks, cleans, makes money, goes to work, goes to school, takes care of the pet, and so on. Ask your child what would happen if, for example, you decided not to do your role. Get your child to brainstorm possible consequences. Then, have your child brainstorm consequences if he or she doesn't fulfill the assigned role in the class (e.g. other kids being angry, a poor grade).

Finally, have your child verbalize exactly what he or she must do in order to fulfill his or her assigned role in class. This is an important step because you want to check that your child understands exactly what is expected. Furthermore, this will make your child 'think' about his or her role. If this is a large problem for your child, think of a reward system that you can create. You can communicate with your child's teacher in order to find out if and when your child will be placed in a group in class. This will enable you to get your child ready for group work by having the discussion in advance.

Gets Angry When Others Make Mistakes

On several occasions, I have seen students raise their voices and get angry at other students who make simple mistakes such as spilling glue, tripping, dropping items, and making spelling and reading mistakes, and fumbling a ball out at recess time.

If your child has a tendency to easily get angry at others who do not do things on purpose, you might want to consider sitting down with your child and discussing the difference between 'on purpose' and 'by accident'. You can start off by discussing with your child what constitutes 'on purpose' (e.g. hitting, throwing objects, and being silly) and what constitutes 'by accident' (e.g. dropping items, reading errors). Make sure your child understands the difference between the two. Have your child give you some examples of thinks that he or she has done both by accident and on purpose.

After, discuss with your child the various ways that he or she should react when someone does something by accident. Emphasize that other children's feelings can be hurt and they can get embarrassed. Let your child know that other kids will be offended by your child if he or she laughs or yells at the other child.

Have your child verbalize a hypothetical situation whereby he or she does something by accident and get laughed at or yelled at. Ask your child how he or she would feel.

Finally, suggest to your child that he or she helps the other child overcome the embarrassment by helping out (e.g. picking up an item, telling the other child it's okay, etc...). Let your child know that this is what good friends do for one another. Your child should also know that even if he or she isn't good friends with the child who had the accident, it is still the proper thing to do and the other child will like your child that much more.

Group Etiquette

One of the most important school social skills your child should master is the skill of listening to and acknowledging the opinions of others in groups.

Group work is becoming a predominant method of learning in the classroom. Students are being taught to work with others so that they are well prepared in the workforce. The ability to 'share' the stage, by listening to and acknowledging others is a skill that must be developed. Quite often, kids only want to hear what they themselves have to say. They are not interested in the opinion of others.

You can help your child become a better listener while in groups at school. First, let your child know why he or she should be listening to others in the group (i.e. the group will do a better job and other kids will want to work with your child because he listens). Let your child know that other kids may contribute important information and understanding to the group which will help your child gain a better understanding and/or grade. Ask your child how he feels when someone listens to him. Tell your child that other people feel the same way when they are listened to. Show your child that eye contact and affirmative nodding signals show that you are paying attention to what the other person is saying. Your child should know that listening doesn't always mean agreeing, rather, it means respecting and acknowledging.

Finally, let your child know that listening makes other kids feel good about working and being around your child and that he or she will have better friendships. Friends and good co-workers listen to each other. The next time your child has friends over watch how he or she communicates with friends. Reinforce and praise eye contact, turn taking, and acknowledgement when listening.

Helping Others

It is common to see that some kids aren't willing to help others. Quite often we believe that these kids are selfish and lack empathy. That may be the case, sometimes, but there is also another reason. Many kids are not willing to help others because these kids lack confidence and self esteem. That is, they believe that they have nothing to offer other people, so, they don't bother.

The negative feelings that these kids are experiencing can be changed. The key is to make your child aware that he or she is liked by others and has skills to offer.

I have used the following technique in my class many times. I call it the "Me Advertisement". It is quite simple and very effective. The idea is for your child to create an advertisement of him or herself. Your child will draw or cut out a picture of him or herself and try to 'sell' his or her abilities. This will allow your child to verbalize, write, and post all of his or her skills and characteristics that can be used to help others. You might want your child to include amiable character traits and skills at home and in the school (e.g. fixing things, drawing, problem solving, cooperating, coloring, giving a helping hand, telling jokes to make someone feel better, etc...).

Try to have your child create a large list of positive traits (see the self-esteem chart in the resource section) and abilities. Have friends and family members help your child with the list. Post the list somewhere in the house where your child can see it on a regular basis.

Includes Others

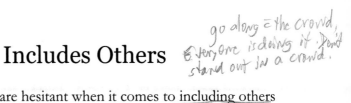

go along ≡ the crowd,
Everyone is doing it. Don't
stand out in a crowd.

Sometimes kids are hesitant when it comes to including others in groups. Kids often feel uncomfortable inviting others in a pre-existing group because of peer pressure. That is, some kids might feel that since other group members don't want to include a new kid in a group, they'll do the same. This can backfire in the future when the kid who succumbed to peer pressure finds himself the victim of exclusion.

Explain to your child that including others gives your child the opportunity to engage in new relationships. It also makes the other kids in the pre-existing group respect your child for his decision. If your child is one of the kids who prefers not to include others, try to show your child how the excluded child feels. Try to get your child to empathize with the excluded child. Get your child to understand that by including others, your child may make a new friend and feel good about himself for doing so.

I have seen this pattern many times in the classroom. Kids are fickle. They gravitate to one group, then another. They exclude one friend one day and another friend the next. Present this concept to your child and let him or her know that if he or she consistently includes others, he or she will find him or herself excluded as well. Let your child know that by always including others, he or she is increasing the chances of inclusion in the future.

Interactions – My Child Doesn't Interact with Other Kids in the Class

It is difficult for you to encourage your child to be more sociable in the classroom since you are not there, but there are some ways that you can actually help from home.

Try to teach your child appropriate ways to interact with other students in the class. For example, tell your child that he or she should take the initiative (see the charts in the resource section in this book) to say hello in the morning, offer to share pencil crayons or other supplies, help other kids with work, and strike up a conversation about a movie, video game, or sport. Suggest to your child that he or she asks other kids to play outside for recess time.

You can ask your child's teacher to try to have your child sit near or in a group with other kids whom you think would be a good match (or who the teacher thinks would be a good match) for your child.

It might be a good idea to have your child try to role play these scenarios so that it will be easier for him or her to carry them out at school.

Interjecting

At school, your child may find him or herself walking into a conversation. Your child, who is excited about a new video game, might interject and start discussing his new game. This is seen as both rude and selfish even though your child had only the purest of intentions.

It is important to let your child know that when he or she walks in on the middle of a conversation, it is always a good idea to listen for a few minutes before entering the conversation. Your child must learn that the group is already involved in a conversation and your child must wait for a break in the conversation or at least until the topic has been changed or finished. Let your child know that it is okay to, for example, discuss his new game, but not if it means interrupting the group's discussion.

You can also suggest to your child that when he or she approaches the group, your child first says hello and says something like, "Excuse me, when you're finished talking there's something I would like to tell you." This is teaching your child how to be respectful and show manners. Furthermore, this gives your child the ability to practice patience and avoid impulsivity.

You can do some role playing at home to reinforce this social skill. Have several family members, or friends who are with you, pretend to be involved in a conversation. Then, have your child make attempts to properly interject. Give your child feedback until he or she properly interjects.

Joining a Group

I can't count the number of times I've had to encourage a student to join a group in the classroom, during gym, or out in the school yard. It's understandable that some children are shy, lack the confidence, and feel like an outsider when it comes to trying to join a group. This situation isn't restricted to new students. In fact, kids who have been at the same school with the same classmates for several years still have difficulty joining a group.

You can try at home to encourage your child to join a group. First, you must make it clear to your child that he or she cannot simply walk up to a group and expect to be asked to join. Unfortunately, this process may take some initiative. Let your child know that he or she must have a plan as to what to say before asking to join the group. One of the biggest problems I have seen is when kids use bragging in order to join a group. They might say that they are the best player, or that the work is easy. Bragging usually turns off other kids. Instead, try to get your child to 'sell' his or her abilities or personality'. For example, your child can approach a group in the classroom and ask to join by mentioning that he can do some drawing for the group. Or perhaps your child might offer to do some research. In the gym or in the yard, your child might want to offer to be goalie first, or to be the first to sit off if there are shifts. The point here is that your child should 'give' something in order to be part of the group. I have used this technique many times with much success. The kids who have used this tactic were quickly accepted in the groups. Then, after a good 'performance' in the group, these kids were asked to join thereafter. One word of caution though. Make sure that your child is not always included in a group because he is always willing to draw or be goalie. Make sure your child doesn't let him or herself be taken advantage of. If this is the case, your child should stand up for himself and realize that his pride and self worth are more important than inclusion.

Keeping Eye Contact

Maintaining eye contact conveys a sense of confidence and friendliness. A child who does not maintain eye contact is seen as lacking confidence, a quality that is not beneficial when making and maintaining friends. Other children might see a child who lacks confidence as weak and unworthy of friendship.

Your child might not be avoiding eye contact with family members because family members are familiar to your child. You may see this when your family interacts with friends or when your child interacts with other kids at extra-curricular activities or at the park. School, especially a big one that is overwhelming, may also be a place where your child avoids eye contact.

If your child does not keep eye contact when interacting with others, you may want to consider finding ways to improve your child's self-confidence. As an educator, and former martial arts instructor, I believe that enrolling your child in martial arts is the best way to improve your child's confidence and self-esteem. If martial arts aren't your child's cup of tea, try putting your child in any other extra-curricular activity that is not competition based. If your child is placed in a position whereby he or she is competing with others, this may undermine your child's already weakened self-confidence. Some alternatives could be: dance, arts and crafts, music, and individual sports.

Also, try to make sure that you don't compare your child with other children in the house. Or, at least, try not to do so when your child is around. Praise your child and focus on his or her abilities. Post and   celebrate your child's accomplishments however small they seem to be. Help improve your child's self-confidence and you will improve your child's social relationships. Lastly, remind your child to make eye contact when he or she does not do so.

Low Self-Esteem at School

Low self-esteem is more apparent at school than it is at home because home offers a child security and familiarity without the pressure from peers. As soon as kids enter the school building, they compare themselves to others and that's when the self-esteem issues change.

Even though you are not in the classroom, you can still help your child raise his or her self-esteem in school and at the same time, help improve your child's social skills. In order to do so, you must be in contact with your child's teacher.

The key here is to take your low self-esteem child's strengths and let him or her show these strengths to others. Let's assume that your child is very artistic, and then with the help of your child's teacher, get your child to tutor a group of kids in art. Or, if your child excels in writing, have him or her be a class leader when the class is editing a story. You will have to discuss this with your child's teacher in advance. This will enable your child to show that he or she is good at something (which raises self-esteem) while at the same time improving social skills (your child will have to communicate with others in a positive manner). If your child doesn't have any clear 'academic' strengths, try to find another strength (e.g. a good peacekeeper, a good leader, a good organizer) that can be utilized in the class.

I have used this strategy in every class that I have taught and have seen positive results. Find a subject area that your child is good at, contact your child's teacher, and have your child be a leader or helper in the class.

Making Friends in the Class

It is hard for parents to help their children make more friends at home considering that parents are not with their children at school. Here are some tips for you to help your child make friends in the class.

- At the beginning of the school year, review appropriate social skills with your child such as: initiating conversation, saying hello, and sharing materials.
- Have your child sit near his or her friends and new students if possible.
- Pick one or two social skills that your child has had consistent difficulty with and work on them before the school year begins.
- Practice social skills just before school resumes after the winter and spring holidays.
- Encourage and reward your child for getting the phone numbers of other kids in the class and initiating play dates.
- Hold occasional 'sleep-over' parties and 'fun outings' whereby your child invites a few classmates.

Nice but Not Too Nice

Let's face it, we all know someone who is too nice and we know what happens to them. They get taken advantage of, walked all over by others, and exploited.

If your child is too nice, it's no different. Your child may be 'too' nice because he or she wants to fit in. By being too nice, your child is trying to get other kids to like him or her. Your child is unknowingly letting others get what they want at the expense of your child generosity. You want your child to be nice and at the same time have self-respect and pride.

When you get a chance, sit down with your child and discuss the difference between being nice and too nice. Use specific examples to demonstrate your point.

For example:

- Let your child know that it is nice to offer part of his snack to a friend but not his entire snack.
- It is nice to let someone take your turn in a game but not for the whole time.
- It is nice to lend someone a toy but not if they don't let you play.
- It is nice to help someone with their schoolwork but not if they copy all of your hard work.
- It is nice to contribute in a group but not if you have to do all the work.

Explain to your child that being accepted is not as important as your child's pride and self-worth. Let your child know that if other kids take advantage of your child then they are not worth being friends with.

To emphasize this concept with your child, you can play a game called 'Nice or Too Nice'. Write down several scenarios whereby your child may be acting nice or too nice. Read out the scenarios to your child and have your child determine if they would be being nice or too nice. Make the game fun; add in a prize or a hug if your child gets the answers correct.

Not Accepted by Peers

Quite often, children who are not accepted by peers have difficulty with social cues.

If your child is not accepted by his or her peers, it may be due to some of your child's behaviors, or perhaps the other children are not the types of kids you would want your child to socialize with.

You can help your child become more accepted by his or her peers (granted the peers are worth the trouble).

- Don't force your child to interact with others with whom your child doesn't feel comfortable with.

- Encourage your child to participate in extra-curricular activities.

- Enrol your child in programs outside of school. Give your child the opportunity to socialize and develop friendships outside the school setting. It may turn out that your child and his/her school peers don't have as much in common as your child will have with peers outside of school.

- Probe into the reasons as to why your child is not accepted. Don't instantly assume that it's everyone else who is the problem. It may be hard to swallow, but maybe your child is lacking in a certain area of social skills. Don't let it affect your ego. Do what's best for your child. Find out the real reason and fix it.

- Be a good role model. Model appropriate social behaviour for your child.

42

- Have your child invite a friend from school over for a play date. Show your child's friend the time of his/her life. Make the experience fun for all (don't overdo it!). Give other kids the chance to see how wonderful your child is. Repeat this with the same friend and then invite other kids over. You will be taking the initiative to help your child develop friendships.

- Try to socialize with family and friends who have kids who accept your child. This will give your child the confidence and essential social skills he/she needs.

Do what you can in order to initiate your child's social interaction. Boost your child's confidence and be supportive.

On Purpose and By Accident

One common difficulty many children with social skills problems have is differentiating between accidents and intentions.

If your child has difficulty differentiating between the two, you can help your child. The best way to start off is to sit down with your child and discuss why accidents happen and what types of actions are intentional. For example, another child may trip and bump into your child. Your child may perceive this as an intentional physical act of aggression when in fact it was an accident. You have to make it clear to your child that he or she has to determine the circumstances. For example, if your child was bumped by another child in the middle of the school yard and no one else was around, there was not ice on the ground, and the other child wasn't playing a sport, then probably, the other child meant to bump into yours. On the other hand, in a busy school hallway or in a cluttered classroom, another child probably 'accidentally' bumped into your child due to the obstructions. Make it clear to your child that different environments and different circumstances will dictate the nature of the 'infraction'.

Have your child make a list of things that could be on purpose (e.g. name calling) and things that are probably by accident (e.g. someone knocks over some books from a desk). Help your child decide which items go under either section of the list.

This understanding will help your child appropriately respond to peers when situations happen in school and at home.

Positive Comments

I remember one year when I was teaching a gym class, a pair of friends almost lost a friendship because of a goal. While playing floor hockey, one boy, the goalie, let in a bad goal. His good friend, who should have given his goalie friend a positive comment, sarcastically said, "Thanks!" Well, the boy in goal was devastated that his good friend put him down.

I called over the verbal offender and explained to him that his friendship is more important than a floor hockey game. I asked him how he would have felt if his friend said that to him if the roles were reversed. The boy admitted his mistake and said that he just got caught up in the game and he didn't want to lose. I asked him what he'd rather lose, a game or a friend. A also asked him what he thought would have been a better comment. He realized that, "Good try", or "Don't worry about it, it's just a game", would have been a better choice.

Even the kindest of kids tend to make negative comments. If you have ever noticed your child making negative comments at home, he or she is probably making them at school as well. Explain to your child how other people feel from negative comments. Brainstorm some positive comments your child can use in various hypothetical situations at school. Finally, remind your child that the feelings of others are more important than losing a game or messing up a piece of work. All those things can be easily fixed but feelings cannot.

Protecting a Friend

Obviously, we want our children to stick up for their friends without fighting. Friendships that are based on two people who also take care of each other create strong bonds. In order for your child to create a strong bond with another child, they both must protect and stand up for one another.

By protecting, I am referring to the protection of one's emotional state (physical protection is part of the equation as well but obviously, I would always suggest that your child seek adult assistance should a physical threat be present). Let your child know that if a child is talking badly about your child's friend, your child might want to consider standing up for the friend. Your child should be polite and say to the verbal bully that he or she doesn't appreciate hearing bad things about his or her friend. Regardless of whether or not your child's friend is present, your child should stick up (verbally) for his or her friend, just as you would want your child's friend to stick up for your child.

This is a life lesson. That is, imagine someone coming up to you and one of your friends and started to insult your friend. Wouldn't you have the instinct to protect your friend? If the roles were reversed, wouldn't you appreciate your friend sticking up for you? We all would. Kids feel the same way. A friend who sticks up for a friend is usually a friend for life.

Teach your child to be smart about it and avoid physical confrontations that don't benefit anyone.

Random Acts of Kindness

There are fewer things people enjoy more than being the recipient of an act of kindness. Not only does the recipient feel good, but the giver feels great about him or herself.

If your child is having difficulties initiating conversation, making new friends, or keeping existing ones, you can help your child by supporting his or her random acts of kindness.

First, let your child know that by being kind doesn't mean that your child should expect something in return. Have your child perform random acts of kindness (daily is too much, once or twice a week would be fine) at school or home. You can create a reward system (see the chart in the resource section in this book) whereby your child will receive a reward for performing random acts of kindness. Before creating the sheet, sit down with your child and brainstorm as many ways as you can for your child to be kind (e.g. giving part of his snack, including someone who was excluded, sharing, picking up a dropped item). You may want to confirm these acts of kindness with your child's teacher.

Respecting Others in School

Having respect for others depends on the amount of respect a person has for them self. In order for a child to learn how to respect others, a child must also be respected. That is, one can only give it if one receives it.

It is important that you discuss with your child that which constitutes respect. Your child should know about respectful words, tone of voice, and actions when interacting with others. If you catch your child not respecting others, make a point of it to stop your child, explain to him what he is doing wrong, and have him correct his behavior.

Also, try to make sure that your child is being respected at home by all family members. Not only should your child be respected with regards to his or her words and actions, but also his or her opinions, wants, and needs. We tend to forget that we must also respect the feelings and wishes of others.

Furthermore, make sure your child understands that other kids come from different cultures, backgrounds, and environments and that your child should respect these differences. Show your child how to appropriately respond to another child who has a 'different' lunch that might not appear appetizing. Or, teach your child how to appropriately respond to different attire, customs, and accents.

A great way to do so is to expose your child to books that have images of different cultures. This will give your child some background information so that cultural differences won't seem alien.

Finally, explain to your child that when he or she doesn't accept others, they feel disrespected and won't want to play with or associate with your child (see the respect checklist in the resource section of this book).

48

Saying Sorry

All kids make mistakes. The difference lies in how they apologize. That is, a child with well developed social skills will be able to look the other child in the eye and say sorry. Kids with poor social skills and/or a lack of confidence will have difficulty saying sorry because they won't be able to look the other child in the face and their voice might not convey sincerity. Furthermore, when a child with poor social skills makes an apology his or her self-esteem will be weakened even more. They might feel foolish or 'dumb' by admitting their mistake.

The first thing you must do is to let your child know that it takes a strong person to admit their mistakes by apologizing. Also, the other child will admire your child more for making the apology because an apology shows that your child cares about the other person's feelings.

Try to role model appropriate apologizing techniques with your child (i.e. eye contact, body language, tone of voice). Another great way to teach your child how to apologize is to be a good role model. The next time you make a mistake at home, make sure your child witnesses your apology.

Seeking Attention

All kids want to fit in and be accepted by their peers. Most kids are able to do so by cooperating, sharing, and playing nicely with others. Kids with social skills difficulties have not yet fine tuned their cooperating and sharing skills. Instead, they attempt to become accepted and try to fit in by seeking attention. Unfortunately, they are seeking attention in negative ways.

Attention is attention, regardless if it is positive (e.g. telling a joke, complimenting someone, showing a new toy) or if it is negative (e.g. pushing people's buttons by teasing, name calling, taking property without asking, or making silly sounds). The end goal from attention seeking behavior is the same, to be accepted.

If you receive notes from your child's teacher stating that your child bothers others, makes silly voices, or blurts out answers in class, then your child is probably seeking negative attention. Your goal is to teach your child to seek positive attention.

Sit down with your child and discuss some of his or her behaviors in the class or at home that are negative attention seeking behaviors. Have your child express to you how other people feel about these behaviors. Get your child to think of alternative ways to get the attention of others. Then, write down both positive seeking attention behaviors and negative seeking attention behaviors. You can then create a reward system for your child (again, see the resource section) for when he or she displays appropriate attention seeking behavior. You can ask your child's teacher to inform you when your child uses positive attention seeking behavior in class.

Finally, if your child is seeking negative attention, you may want to consider finding ways to improve your child's self-confidence. You can enroll your child in a non-competitive extra-curricular activity such as karate or swimming to help your child's self-esteem.

Sharing and Asking for Materials in Class

For such a simple task, many kids seem to have great difficulties properly asking for materials from others in school. Some kids feel a sense of entitlement and rudely ask to borrow something. Other kids are shy and ask with soft voices and without eye contact.

In order for your child to appropriately interact with others in the class (i.e. asking to borrow materials), your child must learn to properly speak to others when sharing materials.

The first skill you must impart to your child is to maintain eye contact with the other child. By avoiding eye contact, your child cannot be sure that the other child was listening. Furthermore, the other child may get the 'impression' that your child is lacking confidence (which may affect future social interaction between the two). Make sure your child always makes eye contact when asking to borrow materials from other kids. Your child should obviously remember to be polite by saying 'please' and 'thank you'. Finally, your child must make sure to use the proper tone of voice when interacting with others. Make sure your child speaks loud enough to be heard. You can practice all of these asking skills at home with your child by doing some role play.

Sharing and asking for materials is an important part of social interaction in the classroom because students often find themselves in this position. By teaching your child how to appropriately ask for materials in the classroom, your will improve your child's social skills.

Shyness

Shyness is a common but little-understood emotion. Everyone has felt ambivalent or self-conscious in new social situations. However, at times shyness may interfere with optimal social development and restrict children's learning.

New social encounters are the most frequent causes of shyness, especially if the shy person feels herself to be the focus of attention. Some children are naturally shy: they are more likely than other children to react to new social situations with shy behavior. Even these children, however, may show shyness only in certain kinds of social encounters. Such children may lack social skills or have poor self-images. Shy children have been found to be less competent at initiating play with peers.

You can help your child overcome his or her shyness. Try to build your child's self-esteem. Shy children may have negative self-images and may feel that they will not be accepted. Reinforce your shy child by demonstrating skills and encourage his or her autonomy. Praise your child when he or she demonstrates extroverted behaviour. Lastly, allow your shy child to warm up to new situations. Pushing your child into a situation which he or she sees as threatening is not likely to help your child build social skills. Help your child feel secure and provide interesting materials to lure him or her into social interactions.

Talking behind Someone's Back

When a student finds out that a friend was talking about them behind their back, that student will become very offended and hurt. He or she will not be able to trust that friend again and trust is a very important part of friendship.

It is important that you explain to your child that it is wrong to talk about a friend (or anyone else for that matter) behind their back. Ask your child how he or she would feel if your child knew that a friend was talking about them behind their back. Get your child to use such words as; angry, hurt, and betrayed.

Let your child know that there is no reason to talk about a friend behind their back. If your child is upset or hurt because a friend said or did something, then your child should take it up with a friend instead of bad-mouthing the friend to someone else.

Let your child know that it is normal for friends to sometimes 'unintentionally' hurt each other. But, when someone talks behind backs, it isn't considered intentional because everyone knows that badmouthing always gets back to the person.

Finally, let your child know that it also isn't right to talk about non-friends behind their backs. This will label your child as some-one who can't be trusted. Let your child know that if he or she talks about other kids to your child's friends, then your child's friends will think that your child talks about them as well. Let your child know that his or her friends won't trust your child and their friendship will be damaged.

I like the following saying:

"If they're talking about you behind your back, you're walking in the right direction."

Trust – Gaining Trust

Gaining trust with peers is essential for the development of solid friendships and new alliances. Children, because they haven't had the numerous experiences of disappointment as adults have, seem to trust other kids automatically. They do so *until* they have a reason not to. Once a child breaks the circle of trust with a friend, it is hard to get back in.

When possible, discuss with your child the concept of trust. Teach your child that trust is keeping secrets and promises. Let your child know that by telling secrets and promises, your child is breaking the trust he or she has with a friend. Ask your child how he or she would feel if your child told a secret to a friend and the friend told someone else. Let your child know that this is how your child's friend would feel if your child did the same.

Explain to your child that trust helps form better relationships. Your child should also realize that once the trust is broken, a friend may not trust your child again. Also, your child should be able to tell you what kind of person is not trustworthy. Make your child aware of the fact that if another child tells secrets that he or she shouldn't or if another child doesn't keep promises, then your child shouldn't trust that child. This may prevent your child from becoming disappointed in the future.

Finally, brainstorm with your child different ways that trust can be broken (see the 'trust' checklist in the resource section). Make sure your child is aware of how to maintain and keep the trust of a friend.

Waiting Your Turn

It's hard for some kids, especially those who are ADD/ADHD or who are impulsive, to wait their turn in a line.

Waiting in a line can create anxiety for some kids. In order for them to release their anxiety, they resort to bothering others, making silly sounds, or even touching other kids in line.

You can tell a child until you are blue in the face to wait for his or her turn but it won't help. The child may understand what you are saying but when they actually get into that line it's a different story.

I've learned a few tricks over the years to help kids wait for their turn while standing in line.

They trick is to get your child to become distracted about waiting by doing something else while still keeping his or her spot in line. Since your child may need to develop his or her social skills, why not do both; keep him distracted and improve his social skills?

Remind your child, on a daily basis, that when he or she is in a line waiting for his or her turn, your child must do either or both of the following.

1. Give a compliment to someone in line.

2. Tell a joke, riddle, or funny story to someone in line.

These ideas will distract your child from the boredom of standing in line and, at the same time, help him develop his social skills.

Part 2-

Social Skills at Home

How You Can Improve Your Child's Social Skills at Home

The following points will give you general guidelines you need in order to implement the strategies listed in this section.

- Work on ONLY one social skill at a time - wait until one goal is successful before you move on to the next goal.
- Reward your child when he makes progress. Rewards can be anything from a hug to a toy to a special play date with a friend.
- Plan a supervised play date for your child to spend with other children in order to practice newly learned social skills.
- Review social goals with your child PRIOR to social outings and play dates. Have your child verbalize the social skills goals and how your child plans on carrying them out.
- Help your child nurture a few quality friendships at a time.
- Collaborate with your child's teacher. Let your child's teacher know which social skills you are working on. Maintain contact with your child's teacher by phone, e-mail, or through your child's school agenda.
- Try to invite your child's friends to your home more often than at your child's friend's home. This will enable you to monitor your child's social skills, as well; your child might feel more comfortable at his or her home base.

Pick a social skill for each week. Use a weekly social skills tracking sheet that is located in the resource section in this book. Pick a social skill and use it for the focus of the week. For example, if your skill of the week is giving compliments, the word 'compliments' goes on the sheet. Then introduce a list of words or ideas that fall under 'compliments'. Have your child brainstorm words and actions that show how to compliment. Throughout the week, have your child fill out the sheet to track his or her behavior. At the end of the week (or month), reward your child if he or she showed a good understanding of the social skill.

Conflict Resolution – At Home

It is easier for you to help your child solve conflicts at home that it is when your child is at school. At home, you can 'coach' your child to successfully resolve conflicts.

When our kids are toddlers, we teach them to be polite and say sorry. As they get older, we should teach them to 'show' that they are sorry.

You can help your child solve problems by incorporating these steps:

1. **Focus on the 1st person perspective.** Kids tend to blame others when there is conflict. When someone is blamed, they get defensive and angry, which perpetuates the conflict even further. Have your child only explain the situation using the word 'I'. For example, instead of, "He took my toy away," have your child say, "I am upset because I don't have my toy anymore". This will keep the conflict from becoming personal, hence more objective for all.

2. **Keep open ears.** Make sure that your child listens to the other person. You can teach your child to wait for the other person to stop speaking. Or, you can make rules such as each person gets to say one thing at a time then the next person gets to speak. It's important for your child to learn to listen in order to better grasp the reason and think about a possible solution to the conflict.

3. **Be a parrot.** Have your child repeat what the other person said. For example, your child had his toy taken from another child. He could say, "I understand that you wanted my toy but I was hurt that I wasn't asked first," This helps the situation in two ways. First, it gives your child some empathy skills, and second, it makes the other

4.

child feel better knowing that his or her feelings were acknowledged (as well, your child's feelings should be acknowledged by the other child).

5. **Agree to finalize.** Finally, have both parties agree on a solution. For example, "Okay, next time, you ask for the toy and I will share it with you. For now, I'm playing with it and you can have it when I'm done."

Remember to be a good role model for your child. When solving conflicts at home, point out to your child the proper way to communicate and find solutions.

Doesn't Take Turns

Most younger children have difficulties taking turns. This can turn into a bigger problem if your child doesn't seem to grow out of this stage.

Whether your child is impulsive, doesn't consider the feelings of others, or both, it is important for kids to learn to take turns. Your child should be aware of the fact that if he doesn't take turns, other kids won't want to play with him (especially if the turn taking involves video games or some other high interest activity). Give your child some turn taking problem solving skills that he or she can use when you are not around. For example, let's assume that your child is having a friend come over and they will be playing video games. We will assume that your child will want to play first and 'hog' the game as long as he can without taking fair turns. Let your child know that he must have a plan for taking turns. For example, you can give your child a timer so that he and his friend switch turns when the bell goes off. Or, they can take turns after completing a level in the game. The point here is that your child should have a 'plan' for turn taking. If there is a plan in place, your child will have the structure he needs in order to take turns.

When this strategy has become successful, have your child verbalize the enjoyment he experiences when he plays with his friends and they take turns.

Finally, you may want to reinforce this behaviour by having a 'turn taking' day or weekend at home. For example, you can designate a day on the weekend whereby your child has to offer everyone else a turn before he takes one. You may want to offer a small reward if your child does this successfully. This will get your child in the habit of letting others go first.

Disagreeing with Friends

This first thing your child should know about disagreeing with a friend is that it is normal to do so. Let your child know that you too have disagreements with your friends and that's okay. In fact, your child should know that we disagree because we all can't have the same opinions about everything.

Let your child know that he or she can disagree using a calm voice and gentle words. If your child becomes emotional during a disagreement with a friend, tell your child to tell the friend that unfortunately they don't feel the same way and that they should respect each other's opinion and stop talking about the issue. Your child may even want to politely tell the other child that he or she needs some space.

You may want to point out to your child that you and your spouse, parents, siblings, and friends disagree but there are no hard feelings (at least not too often!). Ideally, the next time you are disagreeing with someone and your child is around, make your child aware of the disagreement. Point out to your child that you are not angry and that you respect the other person's opinion. Finally, you can show your child how to settle the disagreement by agreeing that you and the other person don't see eye to eye and you want to stop the discussion or by simply talking it out.

Empathy

Empathy means identifying with and being concerned about other people's feelings and needs. It's all about caring for other people. Empathy allows your child to be understanding and tolerant of different points of view and to feel for others.

Empathy is an extremely important character trait because it is the backbone for interacting with others. A student with poor social skills basically lacks empathy because he or she only thinks of his or her own position and neglects to neither take the point of view nor feel for others.

You can help your child become more empathetic by teaching your child to cooperate, include others, and ask others how they feel. You might want to talk about the point of view of others as you watch television, movies, read books or discuss other people with your child. Be a good role model for your child by showing care toward others, such as helping the elderly, the sick, opening doors, carrying items for those who can't, and generally helping others.

Expectations

We all know someone who walks around with high expectations from others. These people often seem disappointed and in conflict. From my many years of experience as a teacher, I can confidently say that this personality trait develops early in life. In fact, I personally and professionally believe that people who haven't fully outgrown their ego and have a strong sense of entitlement. I've met adults and taught children who seem to have very high expectations from friends and always seem to be disappointed in the end.

Firstly, discuss with your child what should and what shouldn't be expected from a friend. For example, your child should always expect respect, understanding, and kindness from a friend but **not** expect to always be included, be given toys, or to be told a secret. Make it clear to your child that there are some universal expectations from friendship. Have your child verbalize to you that he or she understands what should be expected and what shouldn't.

Second, have your child create a 'friend' inventory. I've used this in my classes and kids really seem to take to it because it provides a visual point of reference. Have your child write down a friend's name with two columns underneath. Make sure you go over realistic expectations with your child. Have your child write down all the positive characteristics that his or her friend has on one side and things that your child expects from the friend on the other side. Hopefully, the list containing the positive traits will be much longer than the expectations. Explain to your child that a friendship is not worth losing because of unfulfilled expectations. The less we expect, and the more we appreciate, the better our relationships will be.

Flexibility

Rigid people don't seem to be as approachable and fun to be with as are flexible people. Rigid people want things done their way and rarely bend to the needs and desires of others. Flexible people on the other hand, are seen as 'easy-going' and are generally considered to be better company.

If you feel your child is too rigid and needs some flexibility, you can help by showing your child that there are more than one way to do things. Compromising is essential for strong friendships and other people's wants are just as important.

For example, assume your child and his friend want to play different games. If your child refuses to play his friend's game, or at least the way your friend wants to play it, then you must explain the idea of flexibility to your child. Explain to your child that he must learn to compromise or 'give-in' something to his friend. That is, your child should realize that he doesn't have to do everything his friend wants; rather he should do some things his friend wants or at least some of the ways his friend wants.

Or, let's assume your child is doing a project with other kids. Your child must understand that a project (or any other task) doesn't have to be completed in a particular way (i.e. the task itself may have its own expectations but the way it is done does not). There are more than one way to do things, especially if other people involved want to have a say.

Lastly, your child must not believe that his or her ideas are the only correct ones. Let your child know that if others have ideas or opinions about something or about doing something, your child must be willing to change his ideas and cater to someone else's.

Going to a Friend's House

When your child's friend comes over, it doesn't take long for you to get a good idea about that child's upbringing. Instantly, you can determine if the child's parents spend time teaching the child manners. Does the child properly greet you? Does she take off her shoes? Does she stop and say hello to everyone in the house? Does he share and take turns with your child? These are some socially proper ways to conduct oneself when being a guest in someone else's home. Hopefully, your child is a polite guest. If not, there are ways to help.

Firstly, make sure your child knows how to enter a home and politely greet the family members. If your child doesn't do so, you can practice at home or monitor your child when he goes with you to someone's home.

Before your child goes over to a friend's home, make sure your child knows his friend's 'house rules'. For example, perhaps your family wears shoes in the house and eats food in any room. Not everyone has the same rules. Your child should be aware about his friend's house rules. Perhaps they don't wear shoes in the house and only eat in the kitchen. Your child can either ask his friend about the rules before going over or you can contact the other child's parents in order to give your child the heads up.

Lastly, discuss with your child how he or she can show good manners when at someone's house. Try to get your child to acknowledge such manners as: picking up after himself, cleaning up toys, playing nicely, and putting dishes away after eating (you'll be surprised at how many kids do this in other people's homes but not their own). It might be a good idea to call the other child's parents after your child has visited. Ask the child's parents about your child's performance. Ask for specific information such as, "Did he clean up after himself?" Then, you will have a good idea of what to work on for the next time (if there is anything to work on).

Greets and Responds to Others

From another child's perspective, your child may seem rude by not initiating a greeting or responding to one.

From your child's point of view, a verbal or physical acknowledgement of another child isn't important. Your child probably saw or heard the other child and that was good enough for him.

Your child, in order to improve his or her social skills, should initiate greetings and respond to interactions from peers. At home, show your child how to properly greet a family member when they leave the house and come home. When out in public, make sure to model appropriate greetings and responses to others.

It is important for your child to know that other kids easily become offended when they are not greeted nor responded to. Help your child brainstorm different ways to greet (e.g. wave, 'hello', 'hi', 'good morning') and different ways to respond (e.g. 'no thank you', 'hi', 'thanks').

How to Say "No"

An important social skill that children must learn is how to say 'no'. As simple as it sounds, many children have difficulties doing it properly. Often, kids will answer 'no' with an aggressive tone, inappropriate words (e.g. 'no way', 'uh uh', 'no chance'), or just shake their heads. It is important to teach your child how to properly say 'no' to other people.

First, you should teach your child how to properly rephrase their answer in a more polite way. For example, your child can reply by saying, "Sorry, I'm not able to do that," or "I'm not interested but thanks anyhow". Let your child know that adding a positive statement with a negative reply doesn't hurt someone else's feelings.

Also, let your child know that by nicely saying no, the other person will respect your child's answer and not feel insulted. Let your child know that it's not always *what* we say but *how* we say it.

If your child is having difficulties properly saying no, you can give him or her some practice at home by doing some role playing involving 'no' types of answers to questions.

Imitates Other Kids

There are fewer things offensive to children as being imitated. Kids really seem to take being imitated quite personally.

There are two reasons why some kids imitate others. The first reason is due to 'button pushing'. Kids, who imitate others, want to get a rise out of the other child. Imitating annoys other kids enough to get them angry. This behavior results in 'negative' attention for the 'button pusher'. The child who is doing the imitating is receiving negative attention from the other child.

The second reason why some kids imitate is because they think it is funny and are not considerate (or they don't notice) of other children's feelings.

If possible, try to determine why your child imitates others. If your child notices that other kids get angry but continues to imitate, then your child may be doing it in order to receive negative attention (see the page on 'negative attention'). If your child isn't aware of the feelings of others (or doesn't really pay attention to the other children's feelings) then your child is demonstrating poor social cues.

In either case, it is first important for your child to know that imitating others is rude and disrespectful. Discuss with your child how he or she feels when imitated. Let your child know that other kids won't want to be friends if they are being imitated.

If your child is imitating in order to receive attention, discuss with your child positive ways to get attention (e.g. making funny jokes, helping out) instead of imitating. If your child is unaware of social cues, explain to your child that he or she should look at the other child's face and see how the other child feels when imitated. Some good practice for this skill can be in front of the television. While watching a show, ask your child how some characters are feeling. Ask your child how he or she knows (i.e. facial expressions, body language). It is more important here that you teach

your child to read social cues because imitating is a by-product of the inability to read social cues.

Finally, if your child seems to have a burning desire to imitate others, let your child know that it's okay if both people agree to play 'copying' as a game. Emphasize 'both people'. Your child should be aware that if the other child wants to stop, your child must stop immediately. You can suggest that they have a secret word that indicates the end of the game. This strategy only works if your child is mature enough to stop when asked.

Interruptions

This is a classic ADD/ADHD issue that seems to be very common. Impulsivity, a classic ADD/ADHD characteristic, likes to show its face through thoughtless interruptions.

You can help curb, and with time, extinguish interruptions altogether. Here are some strategies you can use:

- Show your child what he or she is doing wrong. It is important to do so at the exact moment that your child is interrupting so that you can 'catch him in the act'.

- Teach your child when it is the appropriate time to speak (e.g. when two other people are finished speaking or when the teacher is finished teaching or asks for answers).

- Model appropriate ways to wait for your turn to speak. Show your child how you wait for his turn and point it out to your child.

- Explain to your child how his interruptions are unfair to others and show poor manners.

- You may want to create a reward and consequence system for your child; specifically a 'credit' based point system (see the resource section). For example, your child gets points every time he does not interrupt but gets points taken away when he does interrupt. When he gets a certain number of points (on the positive side) he gets a reward. Conversely, if he gets to zero or the negatives (there's a lesson on integers), he receives a consequence.

Keeping a Promise

For some reason, kids are extremely hurt when a friend breaks a promise. In fact, they take it very personally. I have had students tell me that they don't want to be friends with another student because that student broke a promise. It turns out that the student broke a promise last year! Kids find it difficult to trust another student when a promise is broken.

You can teach your child to keep promises, hence friendships. First, discuss with your child what constitutes a realistic promise. Quite often, kids promise things that are beyond their control and when the promise is broken the other child becomes hurt. Tell your child to stop the next time he or she makes a promise to a friend and make sure the promise is realistic and can be kept.

Point out to your child that he or she shouldn't make promises in order to make friends. Let your child know that being friends come first and promises come after. Ask your child how he or she felt when a promise made to your child was broken. I'm sure your child's answer will indicate that he or she felt quite bad. Point out that this is how her or his friend would feel should your child break a promise.

If possible, sit down with your child and go over the difference between good promises that can be kept and unrealistic promises that are hard to keep. Once your child sits down to help you write the sheet and 'sees' the difference between good and not so good promises, he or she will make better promises with friends.

Keeping the Peace

Children with poor social skills often have difficulties following rules and doing what they should do even if there is no adult around.

In order for your child to be accepted by others, your child must follow rules, share, take turns, and cooperate with others at all times.

You should probably have a good idea as to your child's abilities with regards to 'keeping the peace'. By following rules and cooperating with others, your child makes his or her mark within the group. By not following rules or sharing, your child may become excluded from playing with others both in school and at home.

There are several ways that you can help your child learn to 'keep the peace' with friends. Good books and movies are effective ways to show your child how to share and cooperate. Just make sure you point out to your child what the character was do-ing wrong, what the character did to fix the problem, and what the result was (i.e. making and keeping friends). Role playing is also a great idea. You can create hypothetical yet realistic situations whereby your child is placed in a position to share and cooperate. Make sure to give your child feedback so that he or she improves for the next time.

Listening – My Child Doesn't Listen to Others

I am referring to listening here as the act of paying attention to and acknowledging what someone else is telling you. I am not referring to the simple act of paying attention and answering.

One of the biggest problems some kids have is that they don't show interest in what another child is saying. We all want to be heard and acknowledged and you should make that clear to your child. The best way for you to find out if your child doesn't listen to peers would be for you to be present when your child is interacting with a friend. You can do this by having your child invite a friend over to play. Unfortunately, your own interaction with your child won't suffice because kids interact quite differently with their peers than they do with their parents.

Your child must understand that the other child wants to talk and be heard as well. Tell your child that if he or she wants to be friends with someone, he or she must 'listen' to the other person's concerns, interests, problems, and everything else the person has to say. Let your friend know that a good friendship usually involves two people with similar interests. Get your child to find the interests that he or she has with a friend (e.g. sports, video games, music) and talk about those interests. Let your child know that the conversations can't always be about what your child or the other child wants. Also, let your child know that listening involves turn taking. Your child has to make sure that she listens and speaks during the interaction. Lastly, and I am going out on a limb here, consider telling your child to 'pretend' to be interested in new kids that your child may not seem to be interested in. This will give your child a foot in the door to interact with someone who your child may have not considered interacting with before. In this process, your child may find that there are common interests.

73

Listening to Parents

A lack of obedience is a major cause of social skills problems in children. Children must first learn to respect parental commands and requests and then follow them.

Sit down with your child and go over some requests and commands that you make for your child (e.g. clean up room, wash hands before dinner). Make sure your child realizes that your requests and commands should be carried out without questions.

Discuss with your child why you make these requests (i.e. to have clean hands, to maintain a clean house, to help improve grades). Let your child know that you know what is best and your child should help out by following your requests and commands.

Have your child explain to you what would happen should he or she not obey your commands (i.e. nothing would get done, something bad could happen, or your child might do something wrong). Also, you must explain to your child that none of the commands are intended to hurt your child or put him or her in a bad position.

Finally, discuss the concept of respect. Give concrete example of how you and other family members respect your child and that the same respect is expected in return. If you start to give out punishments and take things away because your child is not obeying, you are creating a situation whereby there is a power struggle. This is counterintuitive considering you are trying to create a home where people do their jobs and respect each other.

Meeting People

How many times have we, as parents, asked our child to smile and say hello when meeting someone? For some reason, shyness kicks in, or, our child just doesn't care that much. Regardless of the reason, children should learn the appropriate manners when meeting people.

First, have your child brainstorm times or place when he would meet new people (e.g. at school, at the mall, birthday parties). Then, have your child explain to you why it is important to look someone in the eye when you say hello while meeting them. Your child should realize that by looking in someone's eyes your child is showing interest in the meeting.

Also, have your child acknowledge that it is important that he or she should be polite when meeting people by smiling and shaking hands as well.

Finally, have your child understand that if he or she meets another child and doesn't show an interest in meeting (i.e. avoids eye contact, doesn't smile), then the other person won't get a good impression of your child and will probably not want to be friends.

You can monitor your child's 'meeting people' manners when you are out with your child. If you see your child is not smiling, making eye contact, or shaking hands, nicely remind your child to do so.

Non-Threatening Social Experiences

Large groups can be threatening to children who lack self-confidence. Shy children may therefore benefit from opportunities to interact with peers in small groups.

You can encourage your child to invite classmates over one at a time for special activities. You can also encourage your child to develop outside interests, like music, karate, dance or art, which will provide a natural basis for interacting with other children. Both of these approaches can boost your child's self-confidence and may help him or her start friendships in the process.

If you are inviting your child's friend over for a play date, make sure you have non-competitive games in your home (or at least hide the ones you have). Non-competitive games will make your child's social interaction with his or her friend feel non-threatening because no one is competing to become better than the other. Toys and games that involve creative play and/or cooperation are best in this situation. You might want to purchase art and crafts materials, action figures, or building toys which foster creativity and non-competitive play. Also, going to the park to play is always a great alternative on warm days.

I believe that children should be exposed to competition; after all, the world is a competitive place. But, if your child is lacking in self-confidence, you can help him or her most by focusing on strengths and ignore weaknesses.

Nonverbal and Verbal Communication Skills

Sometimes, children who are very social are perceived as rude because they lack some of the basic nonverbal and verbal communication skills. These kids are sometimes impulsive and/or they don't pay attention to the 'rules' of communication with others. You can help your child improve his or her basic verbal and nonverbal communication skills.

First, make sure your child maintains the proper physical proximity to other kids when talking. Let your child know that everyone has their own personal space. If you notice that your child invades personal space, stop him immediately and let him know. This will get your child used to the fact that 'other' people have their own personal space and it will give him an idea about the size of the space.

Make sure your child orients his or her body when speaking and being spoken to. Often children talk with their backs to others or they turn their bodies when spoken to. Let your child know that when people are talking, they generally face each other (unless one of them is in the middle of doing something). Have your child show you that he or she knows the various gestures that coincide with nonverbal communication such as: shaking the head to show a negative response, nodding, shrugging shoulders to show confusion, and putting up a palm to signal stop.

Finally, make sure your child understands that it is proper to interject when there is a pause in speaking and not at the time when your child wishes to speak. Let your child know that everyone wants to express themselves and they get offended when they are interrupted.

Not Hurting Someone Else's Feelings

Children generally impulsively speak without thinking about the effects of their words on others. They unintentionally hurt the feelings of others.

Make sure your child understands issues that other people may find offensive (e.g. physical appearance, lack of certain abilities, less appealing items). Have your child verbalize to you things that others can say that might hurt your child.

Teach your child to pick up on social cues when someone's feelings are hurt (e.g. sad face, teary eyes, crying). You can discuss this at first, then, try to point it out to your child. You can do so when a family member's feelings are hurt, when a picture book character's feelings are hurt, and while watching television. Ask your child why the person or character's feelings were hurt. Also, ask your child what did the other person say or do to make the person feel bad. Lastly, you can have your child tell you what the person who made the mean statement should not have said or done.

Finally, teach your child the old motto that, 'if you have nothing nice to say, don't say it at all'.

Offering Food or Toys

Sharing food and toys is a social skill that some younger kids must improve. Sharing, though, begins with either asking or offering. Your child will find it easier to share items (i.e. give and receive) by learning how to offer.

First, let your child know that he or she is not always required to share food or toys, but it is a nice thing to do. Make your child aware of the fact that when he or she offers food to consume or toys to play with or borrow, your child will be offered the same by that friend sometime in the future (hopefully).

Second, have your child become aware of the proper way to offer something. That is, your child should hold out the item and ask his or her friends if they want the item. Make sure your child's voice doesn't convey the feeling that the offering is a burden.

Third, make sure your child is willing to give up that item. Often, kids don't think that their friend will take the offer and this can become quite upsetting (you may want to provide your child with extra items if you know that he or she wants to share them).

Finally, be aware of the fact that sometimes, other kids will try to take advantage of a child who always gives. Make sure your child realizes that part of a friendship is 'sharing' and if your child is always offering but never being offered, then, your child should nicely let his or friend know that your child should be offered food or toys as well.

Play Time – Compromising

A common social skill that many children lack is the ability to compromise when playing. As parents, we often see kids trying to get their way by insisting that both kids play each other's game.

Your child must learn that in order to have friends to play with, your child must be willing to play games that his or her friend wants to play as well as what your child wants to play. Let your child know that other children won't want to play with your child unless he or she compromises (you may want to go over the concept of compromising).

Try to brainstorm different ways that your child can compromise with a friend. For example, tell your child that when he or she is playing with a friend, both kids get to choose a game each (or two games…whatever they wish). Tell your child that good friends take turns as to who gets to choose their game first. Or, if your child is not capable of doing so, suggest to your child that he and his friend agree that the guest always gets to choose first.

You may also want to consider giving your child a timer so that he and his friend can evenly divide their play time (or have your child monitor a clock or his watch).

It is important that your child refrains from whining and showing facial expressions of disappointment when his or her friend chooses a game that your child doesn't like. Let your child know that these actions will make the friend feel bad and not want to play.

You may want to consider being present the first few times your child uses compromising skills when having a friend over to play.

80

Phone Etiquette

For a child who has social skills difficulties, or a lack of confidence, it is important to learn how to properly interact on the telephone.

The phone is a great tool for kids who lack in confidence (i.e. many children with poor social skills) because the phone is less personal and doesn't require eye contact and is therefore a good start.

When your child reaches the appropriate age (perhaps 5 or 6 years old), show him or her how to properly converse on the phone. Make sure your child says 'hello' and 'goodbye'. If your child calls a friend and a sibling or parent answers, let your child know that it is polite to say something like, "Hello Mr. Smith. How are you? Can I please speak to David?"

Make sure your child doesn't just get on the phone with the friend and start off with, "Do you want to come over?" Your child should start with a 'hello' first, then get into the conversation.

Using the telephone is a great first step for your child to learn how to initiate conversation with others. Then, when your child gains more confidence, you can begin to improve his or her person to person conversation skills.

Preparing for a Play Date

Before your child has a friend come over for a play date, you might want to consider making a plan with your child in order for your child to work on his or her social skills.

For example, let's assume that your child has to work on his or her turn taking skills. It would be a good time to sit down before your child's friend comes over and discuss the proper ways to take turns. Or, you might want your child to work on sharing, listening, or problem solving. What's important here is that you and your child sit down and make a plan of action. Have your child focus on one social skill to work on because it will be too hard to work on more.

You might also want to consider monitoring your child every so often when a friend is over. This way, you can determine your child's area of needs with regards to social skills. You can choose to intervene or save the discussion for after your child's friend leaves. After your child's friend leaves, it is always a good idea to discuss, with your child, his or her social skills in order for your child to be able to reflect upon his or her actions.

You can use this technique if your child visits a friend's house as well. Depending on your relationship with the other child's parents, you can ask them how your child's social interaction went during the visit.

Again, make a plan by focusing on one social skill; discuss some problem solving strategies with your child, and enable your child to reflect on his or her behaviour.

Pride in Helping

There are fewer things in life that make us feel more proud than helping others, especially a friend. After all, that's a big part of a friendship. By helping a friend, we strengthen the bond and we feel better about ourselves.

By teaching your child to help a friend, you are helping your child strengthen personal bonds, improving your child's self-worth, and giving him or her a sense of pride.

Your child should be aware of the fact that helping doesn't always mean doing something physical. Helping can be simply listening, acknowledging, and trying to problem solve. Go over some hypothetical scenarios with your child with regards to your child helping a friend in need. Ask your child how he or she felt when your child had helped someone. Let your child know that by helping a friend, your child is performing one of the most important behaviors in a friendship. Ask your child how he or she would feel if a friend didn't help. Make sure your child realizes that if he or she didn't help a friend, the friend would feel just as bad.

Try to capitalize on the times that you help a friend. Make sure to point it out to your child. Let your child know how you feel about yourself. Also, ask your child how your friend feels after receiving the help.

Public Places

Your child must be aware that behavior in public places is different from behavior at home. Your child must learn to pay attention to the surroundings and people when out in public.

Make sure your child understands the difference between public and private places. Have your child list off some examples of each (e.g. public – mall, restaurant, private – home). Explain to your child that in public places, your child might have to share space and that space doesn't belong to your child. Your child must realize that everyone shares public places and that your child must be considerate of others.

Have your child brainstorm behaviours that are acceptable in private places and behaviours that are acceptable in public places. Your child should note that shouting, running around, and making noises may be acceptable at home (to some extent) but not necessarily out in public.

Before going out to a public place, review appropriate behaviours with your child to make sure that he understands what is expected. If this is a real problem, you may want to set up a reward system for your child (see the resource section for blank charts).

Reading Faces

Students who have social difficulties are usually unable to determine the emotions of others (i.e. reading faces). This inability to read social situations prevents a child from appropriately interacting with others.

First, try to determine if your child is able to tell if someone is happy, angry, or sad by their facial expressions. That is, have your child verbalize that a happy person smiles, an angry person has narrowed eyes and a tight mouth etc. You can play a game with your child by making faces and guessing the other person's emotions.

You can also have your child practice reading other people's and character's faces when watching television and reading books.

Let your child know that he or she should try to pay attention to his or her friend's faces more often when playing and at school. In order to get your child in this frame of mind, remind your child, just before a play date with a friend, to read the friend's face when playing. If your child forgets, you can establish a visual cue (e.g. when you pull on your ear) for your child to read his or her friend's facial expression. A good time to do this is when your child's friend is very happy, sad, or angry. After your child's friend leaves, have the discussion about your child's friend's emotions.

Responsibility

Being responsible means being dependable and keeping promises. It is accepting the consequences for what we say and do.

Kids who are responsible don't make excuses for their actions or blame others when things go wrong. They think things through and use good judgment before they take action. They behave in ways that encourage others to trust them. Trust is the glue that holds a friendship together.

Your child must come to the realization that when he doesn't carry out his responsibilities at school other kids will resent him and when he doesn't carry out responsibilities at home, family members will become annoyed.

You can help your child become more responsible by creating a reward system. Your child requires incentive to remember to carry out responsibilities at home and at school. At home, you can easily create a chart and track your child's responsibilities (see the resource section at the back of this book for some charts to use). With regards to school, you can contact your child's teacher on a daily basis and ask for regular updates on your child's progress.

Finally, make your child aware that when he doesn't complete his responsibilities when in groups with other kids, then the other kids will get angry because they have to do your child's share of the work. Ask your child how he would feel if he had to do someone else's work because that person didn't want to carry out their responsibilities.

Saying What You Mean

Sometimes kids are afraid of being embarrassed or looking inadequate so they tend not to say what they mean. Quite often, this means that they might agree on something when they know they shouldn't.

Let's say, for example, that your child is having a birthday party but can't decide where to have it. One day, while playing with friends, your child tells the other kids that he wants to have his birthday party at a bowling alley. Another child in the group says that bowling birthday parties are for little kids. Then, the other child asks your child what he thinks. Your child, after looking at the other kids' faces, agrees that bowling birthday parties are for little kids even though your child really wants a bowling birthday party.

Peer pressure plays a vital role by forcing children to not say what they mean.

Your child must learn that it is better to be honest to himself and others and stand up for what he believes in more than avoiding embarrassment or ridicule. Give your child examples of times when you stood up for yourself and were honest even when you felt like caving in to peer pressure. Tell your child that he should say what he means because it will always be for the best (unless it unnecessarily hurts someone else). Furthermore, let your child know that by expressing his or her true feelings, other kids will respect your child's words because they will sense your child's confidence to be honest.

Sensitivity – My Child is Very Sensitive

The problem children have when they are too sensitive is the fact that they internalize what the other person is saying as, "There's something wrong with me."

There is nothing wrong with children who are more prone to being overly sensitive. In fact, I believe that it contributes to a healthier society when children are empathetic. The problem here though, is the question of social interaction. An overly sensitive child may not develop the appropriate social skills. Furthermore, a child who is sensitive may be in need of greater self confidence.

Firstly, reward your child for appropriately reacting to things that other kids say or do. Make a big deal about it. Show your child that you are proud that he/she didn't let words or actions bother him/her this time. Also, have your child express how he/she feels about the situation.

If your child has an older brother, sister, or cousin, have them model appropriate behavior. Your child will see this 'older child' who doesn't internalize everything that is said and done.

When your child overreacts, explain the concept of 'overreacting' and what could be done the next time to prevent it. While doing this, you can teach your child to deal with his or her feelings by expressing themselves.

Find playmates (i.e. neighbors, cousins, family friends) who are a good influence on your child and try to spend more time with these kids. Boost your child's self confidence. Find a skill or activity that your child is good at and make a big deal about it. Stay away from team activities and try to put your child into an activity that is more independent. If your child interacts with others, and sees that others are 'better', your child's confidence will be undermined. Independent activities allow your child to compete against him or herself.

Teach your child the difference between teasing and joking. Sometimes children have difficulty differentiating between friendly teasing for verbal abuse. Make sure your child realizes the difference (see the pages on teasing).

Show your child to focus on improvement rather than perfection. The quest for perfection only leads to disappointment. A child can always improve and improvement leads to confidence.

Lastly, find the things that make your child overly sensitive. Talk to your child and help him overcome his sensitivity by diminishing the importance of those things.

Sharing Friends

Some children have a difficult time when their friend becomes friendly with another child. Jealousy kicks in and fights begin.

Your child must learn that 'friendship' means that the other person has the freedom to play with whoever he or she wishes. Let your child know that just because a friend wants to play with someone else doesn't mean that your child has lost a friendship. Tell your child that he or she can ask the friend to join in. If the friend says no, then perhaps that child wasn't a good friend in the first place. Also, explain to your child that this is why it is good to have many friends (i.e. so that your child doesn't rely on one child and wind up alone should the other child not want to be friends anymore).

Ask your child how he or she would feel if a friend told your child that he or she couldn't have any more friends. Let your child know that friendships shouldn't have these kinds of restrictions. Your child should realize that a good friend is usually inclusive. Your child should also realize that his or her friend doesn't always have to play with your child. Sometimes friends need a break from one another.

Finally, if your child's friend is invited to a party or to play with other kids on the field, suggest to your child to be a good sport about it and not get angry and upset because this will just lead to an argument. Remind your child that his or her friend will play another day.

Swearing

As parents, we cannot avoid our children hearing vulgar language on television and at school. What we can do though, is to teach our kids to use other words to express themselves.

Try to have your child list off some vulgar words that he or she has heard (you can have your child write them down if you please). If your child is eight or older, you may want to hold back on this one as he or she probably knows all the bad ones.

Explain to your child that other people are offended and insulted when they hear swear words. Your child should also know that he or she can get into trouble in school for using such words.

Also, explain to your child that these words are sometimes used in movies or television but are not meant for everyday use. Let your child that using swear words doesn't make your child sound older, instead, it makes him sound less intelligent.

Here are some 'milder' words your child can use:

Milder words for **"shit"**:

- Poop
- Crap -- may not be considered much milder in all areas.
- Crud

Milder words for **"bullshit"**:

- Bull hockey
- Bull
- BS

Milder words for **"damn"**:

- Darn
- Drat
- Rats

If need be, you might want to set up a reward/punishment system for your child (use one of the blank tracking sheets from the resource section). You can create consequences every time your child swears and rewards for every time he either doesn't swear or uses some 'milder' words.

Table Manners

Families have different expectations while at the dinner table. Some families say a prayer, don't place elbows on the table, and some don't allow anyone to leave until all are finished. Others don't really have any rules except that everyone should simply sit down together and eat nicely.

If your child exhibits poor table manners (according to your family's expectations) then you should have your child first explain to you what your family expectations are at the dinner table. For example, you may want your child to verbalize that he understands that he must ask to be excused from the dinner table, not lick the cutlery, or not reach over the table.

When your child understands your family's rules, explain to him why there are dinner table rules (e.g. to show consideration for others, because people will think your child is a slob if he doesn't follow rules, so that no one spills anything).

A great way to point out good manners at the dinner table is to model them for your child. For example, "Jonathan, Did you see how Daddy asked for the ketchup instead of reaching over the table? Do you think you can do the same?"

Make sure to make it clear to your child that these rules also apply to eating at other places such as a friend's house.

Teasing – Appropriate Teasing

Teasing can either be funny and playful or it can be hurtful. It is important that your child understands the difference between the two.

Your child may have a friend who has a nickname. Sometimes, kids with nicknames enjoy the attention they receive. On the other hand, some kids with nicknames are too embarrassed or lack the confidence to tell other kids that they don't like their nickname. Let your child know that he or she should ask the other child if the nickname is fun or hurtful. Then, fun 'teasing' can take place.

Let your child know that there is a difference between laughing **at** someone and laughing **with** someone. For example, let's say another child trips in the hall at school. Your child should be able to assess the situation. If the child who tripped isn't hurt, and is a friend to your child, then your child can have a good chuckle and even make a gentle teasing comment such as, "Did you have a nice trip?" Or, let's say your child is at the water fountain and water splashes in his face. Then, your child's friend approaches and says, "How about leaving some water for the rest of us?" This is friendly teasing. Your child should know that if feelings and/or bodies are not hurt and playful teasing is illustrating that little mistakes are just that. Your child should also be aware of the difference between being teased and made fun of. Let your child know that friendly teasing usually involves funny and non-hurtful truths (e.g. falling, mixing up words, or doing something out of character). On the other hand, hurtful teasing would involve making fun of someone's abilities or laughing when someone is hurt.

Most importantly, let your child know that when someone teases, it usually means that they like your child. Teasing is a way that someone lets your child know that your child's mistakes aren't that important.

Teasing – Inappropriate Teasing

Teasing can also be malicious and, unintentionally harmful. When someone is teased about their appearance, lifestyle, or lack of ability, teasing can be extremely hurtful.

If you think that your child has difficulty discriminating between appropriate and inappropriate teasing, sit down with your child and help him understand the difference. Let your child know that teasing someone with regards to their body size, height, skin color, accent, ethnicity, lack of ability, and disability is considered to be a form of bullying and is not a form of teasing. Calling a skinny person 'stick' or a larger person 'blimp' is mean and hurtful, not funny. Or, calling a kid who lost a race 'turtle' will hurt his feelings.

Conversely, if the fastest kid in the class won and he was given a nickname of 'turtle', he would probably understand that since everyone knows that he is the fastest and 'turtle' is just a joke.

Let you child know that teasing is not always the best choice when playing with friends. Rather, sharing, taking turns, including others, telling jokes, and sharing interests, are better choices when playing with friends.

Telling the Truth

When a child is lied to, he or she will begin to distrust the child who lied. For young people, being lied to seriously affects their ego. Kids who are known to lie usually become outcasts and are excluded from social groups.

The first thing you should do is discuss the act of lying and its consequences with your child. Have your child discuss a situation when he or she was lied to. Have your child express how he or she felt and how he or she thinks other kids would feel should your child do the lying.

You may want to consider consequences for your child should you catch him or her in a lie. Personally, I believe that the most natural consequence is for your child to admit his or her lying to the person he or she lied to. Make sure to have your child explain why he or she lied in the first place (e.g. 'I wanted to be accepted', 'I wanted your approval'', and 'I wanted the attention''). Then, after you find out 'why' your child lied, you can try to help (e.g. if your child is trying to be accepted, you can teach him how to do it properly).

Finally, try not to dwell on the lying, rather, give your child much praise and positive attention for telling the truth. This will give your child the attention, feelings of self-worth, and the acceptance he or she needs instead of the shame and negative attention if you were to focus on the lying.

Tone

"It's not what you say but it's how you say it."

Your child can learn this truth by some good modelling. Pick a phrase such as 'don't touch my toy'. Have your child say this phrase using different tones of voice. Get your child to say it nicely, with anger, with sadness, and several other tones and emotions. This exercise helps your child understand when and how to use a certain tone of voice with the same words. Also, have your child place inflections on certain words in order to get a specific effect. For example, your child can say, "*don't* touch my toy" with an emphasis on the word 'don't'. This emphasis on don't conveys a tone of anger, annoyance, or determination. By having your child say, "Don't touch *my* toy"; your child is conveying a sense of ownership. Finally, if your child says the phrase with a smile and finishes it with a rise in voice, the statement would sound like a gentle command.

Explain to your child that his or her tone of voice can make a difference in how people feel (i.e. an angry tone makes others feel bad). That is, by smiling and using a soft voice, your child can say many things that would otherwise be hurtful if said with anger or a rough voice.

The next time you ask your child to do something at home, make sure your tone emphasizes kindness. Then, point out to your child how you spoke and how he felt.

Using a Cell Phone

It is quite understandable that many children require a cell phone in case of emergency. Most schools have rules that students are not allowed to bring cell phones into the classrooms. The problem though, is that many kids don't use their cell phones in public with any consideration for others.

Your child should be aware of the locations where a cell phone shouldn't be used (e.g. library, in an office, in a line, movie theatres) and where one can be used. Explain to your child that he or she shouldn't be using a cell phone in places where people are working or having their own conversations. Your child should make sure that his or cell phone ringer is not on when in 'quiet' places.

Furthermore, your child should be aware of the fact that it is considered rude to talk on the cell phone when your child is with friends or family.

You may want to consider making some cell phone rules with your child. For example, your child should try to talk quietly when in crowds or go to another room or outside if a call is necessary.

Part 3-

Behavior Charts and Checklists

The following contracts and forms are yours to use as you please. I recommend that you copy, enlarge, and post them in a visible space in your home. Or, you can work right from this book. Most of the charts are blank so that you can make photocopies and use them over and over with different social skills.

You can use one, two, or more contracts at a time depending on what your child can handle. Decide on the behaviors you want most from your child and use the appropriate form. Try not to overwhelm your child. I have included many blank behavior tracking sheets that you can use for any type of behavior.

Social Skills charts can help you motivate your child to change his or her behavior. Sit down with your child and decide on the types of rewards that are fair and give your child incentive.

It is important to:
- Be consistent!
- Create tangible expectations
- Sit down with your child to determine rewards
- Work WITH your child

You may want to set up a token economy in order to improve your child's social skills.

Social Skills Management Program - Social Skills Token Economy

A social skills token economy requires that your child, instead of expecting privileges for doing nothing, now have to earn privileges by getting tokens through appropriate social skills. A token economy is simply a contract between your child and yourself that states that if your child behaves inappropriately, you will agree to trade in tokens for a particular reward or privilege. A token economy can help your child be more responsible and change his or her behaviors for the better.

The process is quite simple.

1. **Choose social skill that you want your child to work on.**
2. **With your child, assign a token value for each behavior.** For example, two tokens for every time your child properly solves conflicts. When your child earns 50 tokens, he can receive a reward. Tokens don't have to be 'tokens' in the sense of money. You can use any tangible object or even check marks. This will give your child ownership of the contract and will make him or her more likely to stick with it.
3. **Be consistent!** This concept relies on both parties (you and your child) following the rules.

Try this type of social skills plan with your child. Make sure that you don't try to change too many social skills at once. First work on the ones that you think your child will find easiest to change. This will give your child more confidence that he or she can change other skills later on.

Social Skills contract between _____

and _____

I, _____, agree to make the following
changes in my social skills:

_____

_____

_____

_____

_____

_____

_____

I know I will be successful when:

_____

_____

_____

_____

When I successfully fulfill my promises in this contract, I
will be rewarded by:

_____

_____

_____

Child signature:

_____

Parent/Caregiver signature:

_____

Parent/Caregiver signature:

_____

Date: _____

My Problem Solving Sheet

Name: _____

Date: _____

The problem was...

_____

_____

_____

The problem occurred at...

_____

_____

_____

I had help during this problem   yes____ no ____

I tried to solve the problem by...

_____

_____

_____

What else could I have done to solve the problem?

_____

_____

_____

Parent/Caregiver Signature_____

_____'s Social Skills Chart

Week _____

Goals
1. _____
2. _____

Day	# of times I reached my goal	Teacher's initials	Parent initials
Mon.			
Tue.			
Wed.			
Thurs.			
Fri.			

Appropriate Social Skills

_____'s social skills tracking sheet

Week _____

My goals	🙂	☹️
Monday		
Tuesday		
Wednesday		
Thursday		
Friday		

Totals for the week _____ _____

My goal to get 20!

My goal is to get 20 stickers by improving…

_____

When I get 20 stickers I will be rewarded by…

_____

I am proud of myself because I was able to…

_____

Race to 30!

| I interrupted | | | | | I waited my turn | | | | |
(put a check mark in a box every time I interrupt)					(put a check mark in a box every time I wait my turn)				
1	2	3	4	5	1	2	3	4	5
6	7	8	9	10	6	7	8	9	10
11	12	13	14	15	11	12	13	14	15
16	17	18	19	20	16	17	18	19	20
21	22	23	24	25	21	22	23	24	25
26	27	28	29	30	26	27	28	29	30

If I reach 30 on this side first I must start all over again.

If I reach 30 on this side first I will be rewarded by…

_____

_____

Race to 30!

_____

(put a check mark in a box
  every time I _____)

_____

(put a check mark in a box
  every time I _____)

1	2	3	4	5	1	2	3	4	5
6	7	8	9	10	6	7	8	9	10
11	12	13	14	15	11	12	13	14	15
16	17	18	19	20	16	17	18	19	20
21	22	23	24	25	21	22	23	24	25
26	27	28	29	30	26	27	28	29	30

If I reach 30 on this side first
I must start all over again.

If I reach 30 on this side first
I will be rewarded by…

_____

_____

I Will Not _____ Today!

Week 1		Week 2		Week 3	
Mon.		Mon.		Mon.	
Tue.		Tue.		Tue.	
Wed.		Wed.		Wed.	
Thurs.		Thurs.		Thurs.	
Fri.		Fri.		Fri.	
Sat.		Sat.		Sat.	
Sun.		Sun.		Sun.	
Total days I didn't _____ this week		Total days I didn't _____ this week		Total days I didn't _____ this week	

I Will _____ Today!

Week 1		Week 2		Week 3	
Mon.		Mon.		Mon.	
Tue.		Tue.		Tue.	
Wed.		Wed.		Wed.	
Thurs.		Thurs.		Thurs.	
Fri.		Fri.		Fri.	
Sat.		Sat.		Sat.	
Sun.		Sun.		Sun.	
Total days I ___ ___ this week		Total days I ___ ___ this week		Total days I ___ ___ this week	

My Friends and Their Good Qualities

Write down the names of your friends. Beside your friend's name, write down his or her good qualities.

My Friends	Good Qualities

My Self-Esteem and Improvement Chart

I am a good friend when I

_____

but I can improve on

_____

I help out by

_____

but I help out more when

_____

I show responsibility when I

_____

but I can be more responsible by

_____

I am really good at

_____

The thing I like most about myself is

_____

Why My Friends Should Trust Me

I think trust is...

_____

I can get people to trust me by...

_____

_____

_____

I don't trust people who...

_____

Trust helps make better friendships because...

_____

_____

_____

The worst way to lose someone's trust is to...

_____

All About Being Kind

I think kindness is...

_____

I can become kinder by...

1. _____

2. _____

3. _____

People will like me if I am kind because...

_____

Kindness helps make better friendships because

_____

_____

_____

3 Random acts of kindness I can perform are...

1. _____

2. _____

List of Compliments

Here is a list of compliments your child can use when in a line, after an argument with a friend, or anytime so that your child can maintain friendships.

You...

...really help me when I need it
...are a terrific reader, writer, etc...
...are a good friend
...are very creative
...are good at soccer, baseball, etc...
...are fun to be with
...make me laugh
...are smart.
...sure know how to...
...are funny
...are trustworthy
...can do anything you set your mind to
...are capable of accomplishing whatever you believe
...are a good listener.
...are very cheerful.
...make me feel better when I'm sad

Cooperation

I cooperate when I

_____

I can cooperate with others by...

_____

I can tell when someone isn't cooperative when they...

_____

It's important to cooperate in a group because...

_____

3 ways I can cooperate in a group...

1. _____

2. _____

3. _____

If I don't cooperate in a group other kids will feel...

_____

because

_____

<u>Honesty</u>

I can be honest by...

_____

I can tell when someone isn't honest because they...

_____

It is important to be honest because...

_____

When someone isn't honest with me I feel...

_____

3 ways I can become more honest...
1. _____
2. _____
3. _____

If I am not honest other kids will feel

_____

because

_____

 <u>Respect</u>

Respect means...

_____

I show respect by...

_____

It is important to be respectful because...

_____

When I don't respect adults I feel...

_____

3 ways I can become more respectful at school or at home...

1. _____

2. _____

3. _____

If I am not respectful other kids and adults will feel

_____

because

_____

Responsibility

Responsibility means...

_____

I show responsibility at home by...

_____

I show responsibility at school by...

_____

I can tell when someone is not responsible when they...

_____

3 ways I can become more responsible at school or at home:

1. _____

2. _____

3. _____

It is important to be responsible at school because

_____

It is important to be responsible at home because

_____

I Got Along With My Classmates Today!

Week 1		Week 2		Week 3	
Mon.		Mon.		Mon.	
Tue.		Tue.		Tue.	
Wed.		Wed.		Wed.	
Thurs.		Thurs.		Thurs.	
Fri.		Fri.		Fri.	
Sat.		Sat.		Sat.	
Sun.		Sun.		Sun.	
Total days I got along this week		Total days I got along this week		Total days I got along this week	

I Got Along With My Siblings Today!

Week 1		Week 2		Week 3	
Mon.		Mon.		Mon.	
Tue.		Tue.		Tue.	
Wed.		Wed.		Wed.	
Thurs.		Thurs.		Thurs.	
Fri.		Fri.		Fri.	
Sat.		Sat.		Sat.	
Sun.		Sun.		Sun.	
Total days I got along this week		Total days I got along this week		Total days I got along this week	

I Kept My Hands To Myself Today!

Week 1		Week 2		Week 3	
Mon.		Mon.		Mon.	
Tue.		Tue.		Tue.	
Wed.		Wed.		Wed.	
Thurs.		Thurs.		Thurs.	
Fri.		Fri.		Fri.	
Sat.		Sat.		Sat.	
Sun.		Sun.		Sun.	
Total days this week		Total days this week		Total days this week	

I Initiated A Conversation Today!

Week 1		Week 2		Week 3	
Mon.		Mon.		Mon.	
Tue.		Tue.		Tue.	
Wed.		Wed.		Wed.	
Thurs.		Thurs.		Thurs.	
Fri.		Fri.		Fri.	
Sat.		Sat.		Sat.	
Sun.		Sun.		Sun.	
Total days I initiated conversation this week		Total days I initiated conversation this week		Total days I initiated conversation this week	

I Didn't Annoy or Bother Anyone Today!

Week 1		Week 2		Week 3	
Mon.		Mon.		Mon.	
Tue.		Tue.		Tue.	
Wed.		Wed.		Wed.	
Thurs.		Thurs.		Thurs.	
Fri.		Fri.		Fri.	
Sat.		Sat.		Sat.	
Sun.		Sun.		Sun.	
Total days I didn't bother anyone this week		Total days I didn't bother anyone this week		Total days I didn't bother anyone this week	

Week 1		Week 2		Week 3	
Mon.		Mon.		Mon.	
Tue.		Tue.		Tue.	
Wed.		Wed.		Wed.	
Thurs.		Thurs.		Thurs.	
Fri.		Fri.		Fri.	
Sat.		Sat.		Sat.	
Sun.		Sun.		Sun.	
Total days _____ _____ this week		Total days _____ _____ this week		Total days _____ _____ this week	

Conclusion

Ultimately, you want to instil the idea that your child should treat others as he or she would want to be treated.

I strongly suggest that you try talking with your child and incorporate the strategies suggested in this book on a consistent basis. If your child still has difficulties improving his or her social skills, then use the charts and contracts located in the resource section as they are very powerful tools for modifying behavior. We all need some kind of incentive to change our behaviours. You know your child best.

Good luck, and

Learn'Em Good!

Stuart Ackerman

Honesty. Compassion. Caring. ... vs   Bossy. Not
Empathy. Good listener.   listening to suggestions,
Patience vs Impulsivity   wants, needs or desires

CPSIA information can be obtained at www.ICGtesting.com
Printed in the USA
BVOW05s1229160314

347744BV00011B/157/P